Selected Works of Aleksandr Bogdanov by Aleksandr Bogdanov
Prism Key Press | www.prismkeypress.com

ISBN: 978-1463694432

The Selected Works of Aleksandr Bogdanov

Contents

Socially Organised Society: Socialist Society

The epoch of capitalism has not yet been completed, but the instability of its relations has become quite obvious. The fundamental contradictions of this system which are deeply undermining it, and the forces of development which are creating the basis of a new system, have also become quite clear. The main features of the *direction* in which social forces are moving have been marked out. It is, therefore, possible to draw conclusions as to what form the new system will take and in what way it will differ from the present system.

It may seem that science has no right to speak of what has not yet arrived and of what experience has not provided us with any exact example. But that is erroneous. Science exists precisely for the purpose of *foretelling* things. Of what has not yet been experienced it cannot, of course, make an exact forecast, but if we know generally what *exists* and in *what direction it is changing* then science *must* draw the conclusions as to what it will change into. Science must draw these conclusions in order that men may adapt their actions to circumstances, so that instead of wasting their efforts by working against the future and retarding the development of new forms, they may consciously work to hasten and assist such development.

The conclusions of social science with regard to future society cannot be exact because the great complexity of social phenomena does not permit, in our times, of their being completely observed in all details, but only in their main features, and for that reason the picture of the new system also can only be drawn in its main outlines; but these are the *most important considerations* for the people of the present day.

The history of the ancient world shows that human society

may sometimes regress, decline, and even decay; the history of primitive man and also that of several isolated Eastern societies shows the possibility of a long period of stagnation. For this reason, from a strictly scientific point of view, the transition to new forms must be accepted conditionally. New and higher forms will appear only in the event of a *society progressing further in its development* as it has progressed up till now. There must be sufficient cause, however, for regression or stagnation, and these cannot be indicated in the life of modern society. With the mass of contradictions inherent in it, and the impetuous process of life which they create, there cannot be stagnation. These inherent contradictions could cause retrogression only in the event of the absence of sufficient forms and elements of development. But such elements exist, and these very contradictions develop and multiply them. The productive power of man is increasing and even such a social catastrophe as a world war only temporarily weakens it. Furthermore an enormous class in society growing and organising is striving to bring about these new forms. For this reason there are no serious grounds for expecting a movement backwards. There are immeasurably more grounds for believing that society will continue along its path and create a new system which will destroy and abolish the contradictions of capitalism.

1. Relation of Society to Nature

The development of machine technique in the period of capitalism acquired such a character of consecutiveness and activity that it is quite possible to determine its tendencies and consequently the further result of its development.

With regard to the first part of the machine – the source of motive power – we have already indicated the tendency, viz., the transition from steam to electricity, the most flexible, the most plastic, of all the powers of nature. It can easily be produced from all the others and be converted into all the others; it can be divided into exact parts and transmitted across enormous distances. The inevitable exhaustion of the main sources of steam power, coal and oil, leads to the necessity for the transition to electricity, and this will create the possibility of making use of all waterfalls, all flowing water (even the tides of the oceans), and the intermittent energy of the wind which can be collected with the aid of accumulators, & c. A new and immeasurably rich source of electrical energy, infinitely superior to all other sources of .electrical energy, has also been indicated, viz., atomic energy, which is contained in all matter. Its existence has been scientifically proved, and its use even begun, although in a very small scale where it automatically releases itself *(e.g.* radium and other similar disintegrating elements). Methods for systematically releasing this energy have not yet been discovered; the new higher scientific technique will probably discover these methods and united humanity possess inexhaustible stocks of elemental power .

With regard to the transmitting mechanism we also observe a tendency towards the *automatic type* of machine. Following this we observe an even higher type – not only an automatically acting, but an *automatically regulating* machine. Its beginnings lie on the one hand in the increasing application of mechanical regulators to present-day machines, and on the other in the few mechanisms of this type already created by military technique *(e.g.,* self-propelling submarines and air torpedoes). Under capitalism these will hardly find application for peaceful production: they are disadvantageous from the point of view of profits as they are very complicated and unavoidably dear; the amount of labour which they save in comparison with machines of the former type is not great, because automatic machinery also dispenses with a considerable amount of human labour. Furthermore the workers required to work them must possess the highest intelligence; hence their pay also would have to be high, and their resistance to capital would be considerably greater. In war there is no question of profits, and for that reason these obstacles to their application do not arise. Under socialism the question of profits will disappear in production also; first

9

consideration will be given to the technical advantages of self-regulating mechanism – which will render possible the achievement of a rapidity and exactness of work incomparably greater than that achieved by human organs, which work more slowly and with less precision, and moreover are subject to fatigue and error.

Furthermore, the number of machines, and the sum total of mechanical energy, will increase to such a colossal degree that the physical energy of men will become infinitesimally small in comparison. The powers of nature will carry out the executive work of man – they will be his obedient dumb slaves, whose strength will increase to infinity.

The technique of communication between men is of special significance. The rapid progress in this connection observed at the end of the capitalist epoch has been obviously directed to the abolition of all obstacles which nature and space place in the way of the organisation and compactness of humanity. The perfection of wireless telegraphy and telephony will create the possibility for people to communicate with each other under any condition, over any distance, and across all natural barriers. The increase in the speed of all forms of transportation brings men and the products of their labour more closely together than was ever dreamed of in the past century. And the creation of dirigible aircraft will make human communication completely independent of geographical conditions – the structure and configuration of the earth's surface.

The first characteristic feature of the collective system *is the actual power of society over nature, developing without limit on the basis of scientifically-organised technique.*

2. The Social Relations of Production

As we saw, machine technique in the period of capitalism changes the form of co-operation in two ways. In the first place, the technical division of labour loses its "specialised" character, which narrows and limits the psychology of the workers, and reduces itself to "simple co-operation," in which the workers carry out similar work, and in which the "specialisation" is transferred from the worker to the machine. Secondly, the framework of this co-operation is extended to enormous proportions; there arise enterprises which embrace tens of thousands of workers in a single organisation.

We must suppose that both these tendencies will proceed considerably further under the new system than under machine capitalism. The differences in the specialisation in various industries will be reduced to such insignificant proportions that the psychological disunity created by the diversity of employments will finally disappear; the bonds of mutual understanding and the community of interest will unrestrainedly expand on the basis of the community of vital interests.

At the same time organised labour unity will grow accordingly, grouping hundreds of thousands and even millions of people around a common task.

The continuation of the development of the two previous tendencies will give rise to two new features of the post-capitalist system. On the one hand, the last and most stubborn form of specialisation, viz., the division between the organisational and executive functions, will be transformed and lose its significance. On the other hand, all labour groupings will become more and more mobile and fluid.

Although in the epoch of machine capitalism executive labour at the machines approaches in character to that of organisational labour, nevertheless a difference between them remains, and for that reason the individualisation of the functions of the executor and the organiser remains stable. The most experienced worker in machine production is very different from his manager, and cannot replace him. But the further increase in the complexity and precision of machinery and at the same time the increase in the general intelligence of the workers must eventually remove this difference. With the transition to the automatic regulators, the work of a simple worker approaches nearer and nearer to that of the engineer, and acquires the character of watching the proper working of the various parts of the machine. If automatic regulators are attached to machines there is no need for the mechanic continually to watch his gauges and indicators to see whether the required amount of steam pressure or electrical current is maintained. All he then has to do is from time to time to see whether the regulators are in working order, to alter them as occasion requires, and to see to their speedy repair when necessary, & c. At the same time the knowledge, understanding, ingenuity, and general mental development required of the worker increase. It is not only practical common sense that is required, but exact scientific knowledge of the mechanism, such as only the organising intellectual possesses to-day. Consequently the difference between the "executor" and the manager will be reduced to a purely quantitative difference in scientific training; the worker will then carry out the instructions of a better informed and more experienced comrade rather than blindly subordinate himself to a power based upon knowledge inaccessible to him. The possibility will thus be created of replacing an organiser by any worker and *vice versa.* The labour inequality of these two types will disappear and they will merge into one.

With the abolition of the last survivals of mental "specialisation" the necessity and the sense of binding certain persons to certain particular work will also disappear. On the other hand the new form of labour will require mental flexibility and diversity of experience, for the maintenance of which it will be necessary that the worker from time to time change his work, going from one kind of machine to another, from the function of "organiser" to that of "executor" and *vice versa.* And the progress of technique, more. rapid than in our day, with its continual improvements of machines and contrivances, must make the rapidly-changing grouping of human forces and individual labour systems, or "enterprises" as we call them to-day, to a high degree more mobile.

All this will become possible and realisable owing to the fact that production is *consciously and systematically organised by society as a whole*. On the basis of scientific experience and labour solidarity there will be created a general all-embracing organisation of labour. The anarchy which in the epoch of capitalism disunites individual enterprises by ruthless competition and whole classes by stern struggle will be abolished. Science indicates the path to such organisation and devises means for carrying it out, and the combined force of the class-conscious workers will realise it.

The scale of the organisation must from the very beginning be world-wide or nearly so, in order that it may not be dependent in its production and consumption upon exchange with other countries which do not enter it. The experience of the world war and the revolutions that followed it shows that such dependence will immediately be converted into a means of destroying the new system.

The type of organisation cannot be other than centralised; not, however, in the sense of the old authoritarian centralism, but in the sense of a scientific centralism. Its centre should be a gigantic *statistical bureau* based on exact calculation for the purpose of distributing labour power and instruments of labour.

The motive force of the organisation at first, *i.e.,* as long as the whole of society has not yet been trained in the spirit of collective labour, will be comradely discipline, including an element of compulsion, from which society will step by step emancipate itself.

In this system of production each worker will be actually on an equality with the rest as conscious elements of one sensible whole; each one will be given all the possibilities for completely and universally developing his labour power, and the possibilities of applying it to the advantage of all.

Thus the characteristic features of the socialist society are *the homogeneous organisation of the whole productive system, with the greatest mobility of its elements and groupings, and a highly developed mental equality of the workers as universally developed conscious producers* .

3. Distribution

Distribution generally represents an essential part of production, and in its organisation is wholly dependent upon it. The *systematic* organisation of production presupposes a *systematic* organisation of distribution. The supreme organiser in both these spheres will be society as a whole. Society will distribute labour and also the product of that labour. This is the very opposite of the anarchic unorganised distribution which is expressed in exchange and private property conducted on the basis of competition and the crude conflict of interests. The social organisation of production and distribution presupposes also the social ownership of the means of production and the articles of consumption created by social labour, until society hands them over to the individual for his personal use. "Individual property" commences in the sphere of consumption which essentially is individualistic. This, of course, has nothing in common with capitalist private property, which is primarily the private ownership of means of production; but does not represent the right of the worker to the necessary means of existence.

The principle of distribution arises directly out of the basis of co-operation. As the system of production is organised on the basis that it secures to every member of society the possibility of the complete and universal development of his labour power and the possibility of applying it for the use of all, so the system of distribution should give him the articles of consumption necessary for the development and application of labour power. With regard to the method by which this is to be achieved, two phases may also be foreseen. At first, when the scale of production is not particularly great, and collectivism has not yet penetrated the spirit of every member of society, so that the elements of compulsion must yet be preserved, distribution will serve as a means of discipline: each one will receive a quantity of products in proportion to the amount of labour he has given to society. Later on, when the increase of production and the development of labour co-operation renders such careful economy and compulsion unnecessary, complete freedom of consumption will be established for the worker. Giving society all that he is able in strength and ability, society will give him all that he needs.

The complexity of the new method of organising distribution must obviously be enormous and demand such developed statistical and informative apparatus as our epoch is far from having achieved. But even in our time the elements exist in various spheres of economic life which should serve as the material for such apparatus. In the sphere of banking and credit, for instance, there are the agencies and committees of experts for studying the state of the market, stock exchange organisation, & c.; in the labour movement, there are mutual aid societies, co-operative societies; and organised by the State are schemes of insurance, & c. All these will have to be radically reformed before they can serve for the future system of distribution, because at present they are wholly adapted to the anarchical system of capitalism and therefore subordinated to its forms. They may be described as the scattered rudimentary *prototypes* of the future harmonious system of distribution.

4. Social Ideology

The first feature of the social psychology of the new society is its *socialness,* its spirit of collectivism, and this is determined by the fundamental structure of that society. The labour compactness of the great human family, and the inherent similarity in the development of men and women, should create a degree of mutual understanding and sympathy of which the present-day solidarity of the class-conscious elements of the proletariat, the real representatives of future society, is only a weak indication. A man trained in the epoch of savage competition, of ruthless economic enmity between groups and classes, cannot imagine the high development between men of comradely ties that will be organically created out of the new labour relations.

Out of the real power of society over external nature and social forces there follows another feature of ideology of the new world, viz., the *complete absence of all fetishism*, the purity and clearness of knowledge and the emancipation of the mind from all the fruits of mysticism and metaphysics. The last traces of natural fetishism will disappear, and this will reflect the final overthrow of both the domination of external nature over man and the social fetishism reflecting the domination of the elemental forces of society; the power of the market and competition will be uprooted and destroyed. Consciously and systematically organising his struggle against the elements of nature, social man will have no need for idols which are the personification of a sense of helplessness in the face of the insuperable forces of the surrounding world. The unknown will cease to be unknown because the process of acquiring knowledge – systematic organisation on the basis of organised labour – will be accompanied by a consciousness of strength, a sense of victory, arising from the knowledge that in the living experience of man there are no longer any spheres surrounded by impenetrable walls of mystery. *The reign of science* will begin and put an end to religion and metaphysics for ever.

As a result of the combination of these two features we get a third feature, viz., the *gradual abolition of all standards of compulsion* and of all elements of compulsion in social life.

The essential significance of all the compulsory standards – custom, law, and morals – consists in the regulation of the vital contradictions between men, groups, and classes. These contradictions lead to struggles, competitions, enmity, and violence, and arise out of the unorganised state and anarchy of

16

the social whole. The standards of compulsion which society, sometimes spontaneously and sometimes consciously, has established in the struggle with the anarchy and the contradictions have become a fetish, *i.e.*, an *external* power to which man has subjected himself as something higher, standing *above* him, and demanding worship or veneration. Without this fetishism compulsory standards would not have the power over man to restrain the vital contradictions. The natural fetishist ascribes a divine origin to authority, law, and morals; the representative of social fetishism ascribes the origin to the "nature of things"; both mean to ascribe to them an absolute significance and a higher origin. Believing in the high and absolute character of these standards, the fetishist subjects himself to them and maintains them with the devotion of a slave.

When society ceases to be anarchical and develops into the harmonious form of a symmetrical organisation, the vital contradictions in its environment will cease to be a fundamental and permanent phenomenon and will become partial and casual. Compulsory standards are a kind of "law" in the sense that must regulate the repeated phenomena arising out of the very structure of society; obviously under the new system they will lose this significance. Casual and partial contradictions amidst a highly-developed *social sense* and with a highly-developed *knowledge* can be easily overcome without the aid of special "laws" compulsorily carried out by "authority." For instance, if a mentally-diseased person threatens danger and harm to others, it is not necessary to have special "laws" and organs of "authority" to remove such a contradiction; the teachings of science are sufficient to indicate the measures by which to cure that person, and the social sense of the people surrounding him will be sufficient to prevent any outbreak of violence on his part, while applying the minimum of violence to him. All meaning for compulsory standards in a higher form of society is lost for the further reason that with the disappearance of the social fetishism connected with them they also lose their "higher" form.

Those who think that the "State form," *i.e.*, a legal organisation, must be preserved in the new society because certain compulsory laws are necessary, like that requiring each one to work a certain number of hours per day for society, are mistaken. Every State form is an *organisation of class domination* and this cannot exist where there are no classes. The distribution of labour in society will be guaranteed on the one hand by the teachings of science and those who express them – the technical organisers of labour acting solely in the name of science, but having no power – and on the other by the power of the social sense which will bind men and women into one labour family by the sincere desire to do everything for the welfare of all.

Only in the transitional period, when survivals of class contradictions still exist, is the State form at all possible in the "future State." But this State is also an organisation of class domination; only it is the domination of the proletariat, which will abolish the division of society into classes and together with it the State form of society.

5. Forces of development

The new society will be based not on exchange but. on *natural self-sufficing* economy. Between production and consumption of products there will not be the market, buying and selling, but consciously and systematically organised distribution.

The new self-sufficing economy will be different from the old primitive communism, for instance, in that it will embrace not a large or a small community, but the whole of society, composed of hundreds of millions of people, and later of the whole of humanity.

In exchange societies the forces of development are "relative over-population," competition, class struggle, *i.e.*, in reality the *inherent* contradictions of social life. In the self-sufficing societies referred to above, tribal and feudal societies, & c., the forces of development are based upon "relative over-population," *i.e.,* the *outward contradictions* between nature and society, between the demands for the means of life arising out of the growth of the population and the sum of these means which nature in a given society can supply.

In the new self-sufficing society the forces of development will also lie in the *outward contradictions* between society and nature, in the very process of struggle between society and nature. Here the slow process of over-population will not be required to induce man still further to perfect his labour and knowledge: the needs of humanity will increase in the very process of labour and experience. Each new victory over nature and its mysteries will raise new problems in the highly-organised mentality of the new man, sensitive to the slightest disturbance and contradiction. Power over nature means the continual accumulation of the energy of society acquired by it from external nature. This accumulated energy will seek an outlet and will find it in the *creation* of new forces of labour and knowledge.

It is true that accumulated energy does not always lead to creativeness; it may lead to degeneration. The parasitic classes of modern, as of former, societies accumulate energy at the expense of the labour of others and seek an outlet for it not in creativeness but in debauchery, luxury, perversity, and refinement. This leads to the weakening of the mentality and to the decline of these classes. But these are only *parasites;* they do not live in the sphere of socially useful labour , but almost entirely in the sphere of consumption. Naturally they seek new forms of indulgence in this sphere and find them in perversity and subtle refinements. But socialist society does not know of such parasites. In it all are workers, and they will satisfy their desire for creativeness arising out of the excess of energy in the *sphere of labour.* They will perfect technique and consequently perfect themselves.

The new forces of development arising out of the struggle with nature and of the labour experience of man operate the more strongly and rapidly the wider and more complex and diverse this experience is. For this reason, in the new society with its colossally wide and complex system of labour, with its numerous ties uniting the experience of the most diverse (although *equally* developed) human individualities, the forces of development must create such rapid progress as we in our day can hardly imagine. The harmonious progress of future society will be much more intensive than the semi-spontaneous progress, fluctuating between contradictions, of our epoch.

All *economic obstacles* to development will be abolished under the new system. Thus, the application of machinery, which under capitalism is determined by considerations of *profit,* under the new system will depend entirely upon *productivity.* As we have seen, machinery which may be very useful for saving labour is very frequently useless from the standpoint of capitalist profits. In socialist society such a point of view will not prevail and there will therefore be no obstacles to the application of labour-saving machinery.

The forces of development which will dominate at this stage will not be new forces; they will have operated previously. In the natural self-sufficing system, however, these forces were suppressed by the general conservatism prevailing in it; under capitalism they are suppressed by virtue of the fact that the classes which take for themselves the product of surplus labour, *i.e.,* the main source of the forces of development of society, do not participate in the *direct* struggle with nature, do not conduct industry personally, but through others, and consequently remain outside the influence of the forces created in the struggle.

Under socialism, however, the sum total of surplus labour will be employed by the whole of society and every member will directly participate in the struggle against nature. Consequently the main and greatest driving force of progress will act unhindered and at top speed, not through a select minority, but through the whole of humanity, and the sphere of development must increase unceasingly.

Thus the general characteristics of the socialist system, the highest stage of society we can conceive, are: *power over nature, organisation, socialness, freedom, and progress.*

Proletarian Poetry

It should be noted that the poetry of the bourgeois world still preserves a great deal of the authoritative consciousness, because bourgeois society has preserved also many elements of authoritative collaboration, of authority and subordination. The variety of the bourgeois groups — big capitalists and petty ones, higher intellectuals, landowners, backward and progressive, stock exchange speculators, renders, &c., together with the different intermixtures and combinations of these groups — naturally gives rise to a variety of forms and subject matter in their poetry, but the basic type is general for all of them.

In machine production the fundamental divergences in the nature of labour begin to disappear. The "working hands" are no longer merely hands, the worker is not a passive mechanical performer. He is subordinated, but he also *rules* his "iron slave" — the machine. The more complicated and perfect the machine, the more his labour is reduced to observation and control. The worker must know all the aspects and conditions of the work of his machine, and interfere in its motion only when necessary; while, at the inevitable moments of caprice or derangement on the part of the machine, he must be capable of quick perception, initiative, and resolution. All these are fundamental and typical traits of organisational work, and for them one must possess knowledge, intelligence, the capacity for exerted attention, which are the traits of the organiser. But there still remains the physical effort; together with the brains, the hands also have to work.

At the same time sharp distinctions between the workers also begin to disappear; specialisation is transferred from them to the machines, the work at different machines is in its essential organisational contents almost the same. Thus there is room for contact and mutual understanding in work done in common, an opportunity to assist each other with counsel and action. Here is the origin of that fellowship in collaboration which is the basis upon which the proletariat constructs all its organisation.

This form of labour is characterised by the fact that organisational work is closely connected with execution. Here the organiser and the executor are not individual persons, but *collectivities.* Things are discussed and solved in common, and executed in common; everyone takes part in working out the collective will and in its accomplishment. Organisation is accomplished not through authority and subordination; instead of these there is fellowship, initiative, and management on the part of all, fellowship discipline controls every individual.

There have been germs of fellowship collaboration before, but only in our epoch has it become a primary type of organisation of a whole class. It grows in depth to the degree of the development of technique; it grows in width in the degree that the proletarian masses are gathered in the cities, to the extent that they are concentrated in gigantic enterprises.

This concentration of the proletariat in the cities and factories has a great and complicated influence upon the psychology of the masses. It contributes to the development of the consciousness that in labour, in the struggle against the elements for existence, the individual is only a link in a great chain and, taken separately, would be a powerless plaything of external forces, a shred of fabric cut from a mighty organism and unable to survive alone, The individual "ego" is reduced to its actual dimensions, its proper place.

But while the masses are gathered in the cities, they become removed from nature. The latter reveals itself to the proletariat only as a force in production, not as a source of live impressions. At the same time city life affords the proletariat very few joys and amusements, however many it may give to the ruling classes; and so the workers' longing for live nature becomes greater, a longing which sometimes passes into a feeling of anguish. This is also one of the reasons for his dissatisfaction, for his struggle to organise new forms of life.

Comradely collaboration is not a ready-made form — it is in a state of development, and has reached different stages in different places. It is followed by the consciousness of fellowship, which is, however, of slower development. This is the primary line of the course of the proletariat. But it is still far from accomplishment even in the most advanced countries. Its accomplishment will be Socialism, which is nothing else than a fellowship organisation of the whole life of society.

The spirit of authority, the spirit of individualism, the spirit of fellowship, these are the three consecutive types of culture. Proletarian poetry belongs to the third, the highest phase.

The spirit of authority is strange to proletarian poetry, it cannot help but be hostile. The proletariat is a subordinated class, and is struggling against subordination.

However, the proletariat is a young class, and its art is still in the stage of childhood. Even in politics, where their experience is greater, millions of the proletarians of Germany, England, and America still follow in the wake of the bourgeoisie. This may happen all the more easily to proletarian poets. So far the poetry of workers is, for the most part, not real poetry. This is not due to the individuality of the author, but to the viewpoint. The poet may not even belong to the working class by his economic position; but if he has become deeply familiarised with the collective life of the proletariat, if he has actually and sincerely become imbued with its strivings, ideals, with its way of thinking, if he exults in its joys and suffers in its sorrows, if, in a word, he has fused his soul with that of the proletariat, then he may be able to give the proletariat artistic expression, he may become the organiser of its forces and its consciousness in poetic form. Of course, this can very seldom happen, and in poetry, as in politics, the proletariat should not count upon allies outside its ranks.

A small prose-poem by a worker — a poet and economist:

Whistles

When the morning whistles resound over the workers' suburbs, it is not at all a summons to slavery. It is the song of the future.
There was a time when we worked in poor shops and started our work at different hours of the morning.
And now, at eight in the morning, the whistles sound for a million men.
A million workers seize the hammers at the same moment.
Our first blows thunder in accord.
What is it that the whistles sing?
It is the morning hymn to unity.

From "The Song of the Workers' Blow," by A. Gastev.

This is lyrical poetry, but it is not the poetry of the individual "ego." For the worker as an individual the whistle is, of course, a reminder of his involuntary labour, it is sometimes even a torturing sensation. But for the growing commune its significance is quite different. The actual creator of the poetry, expressing itself through the poet, is not the same as before, and the things it finds in life are also different. It is the spirit of fellowship.

The investigator most have a foothold in reality. We were in a difficult position at one time, as the few enthusiasts for proletarian art, when we had to speak of things which could not be found in life, when we could not say clearly : "Here, this is real proletarian art; by this model you may judge, with this you may compare." And I must cite here the poem in which I personally found my foothold.

In the year 1913 there was printed in the *Pravda* a little poem of Samobitnik:

To a New Comrade

See the wheels that whirl around,
See the mad belts dancing here ...
Comrade, comrade, have no fear!
Let the chaos of steel resound,
Though its many fires be drowned,
Quenched by bitter sea of tears —
Have no fear!

You have come from peaceful haunts,
Quiet fields and brooklets clear.
Comrade, comrade, have no fear!
Here the limitless is bound,
Here the impossible come round ...
This is the dawn of coming years —
Have no fear!

Foaming crests of waves resound
With our fortune coming near. ...
On our kingdom gloomy, drear,
A new sun is shining down,
Burning brighter now than e'er
Have no fear!

Like a giant carved in stone
At the mad belts stand and steer..
Let the wheels go turning still,
Closer now the ranks are drawn —
You're a new link forged in here-
Have no fear!

It is not the artistry that interests us most in this poem. What is most striking is the purity of the contents. I doubt whether one could be more proletarian in feeling and thought.

The thing happened during the old *régime*. A new worker has come to the factory straight from the village. What is he to

27

the old habitual worker? A competitor, and a most inconvenient one, too: for he lowers the wages, his demands are smaller, and he can hardly assist in the general cause since he is unable to defend even his own interests. Of the general cause he has no idea at all. His thought is slow, his feelings narrow, his will limited, his heroism small .... It is hard to rely on him should there arise a need for concerted action. But observe the attitude of his fellow-worker, the poet, towards him, the strange newcomer. With what chivalrous attention, with what gentle care, he encourages the timid novice and leads him into a world which is unknown, incomprehensible, strange, and even fearful to him! With what simplicity and force, in few words, but with clear images, the poet tells him all that he should know and feel in order to become a comrade among comrades : he draws for him the picture of the gigantic forces of the "steel chaos" of modern technique, he tells him the bitter truth about the "sea of tears" which it costs humanity, and the joyous tidings of the "new sun" of the great ideal, of the proud fortune of common strife. Touching is the recollection of the wonderful far-off nature, of the peaceful haunts, "quiet fields and brooklets clear" amidst stone and iron — the heart of the proletarian is longing for nature, but it is seldom that he gets the joy of meeting with her. But everything will be accomplished by the growing, steady, irresistible effort of the collective creative will .... Victorious confidence sounds in the concluding lines:

> Closer now the ranks are drawn —
> You're a new link forged in here —
> Have no fear!

It is the introduction of a new brother into the knighthood of the Socialist ideal.

Well, is not the poet the organiser of his class?

Proletarian poetry is still in its embryo stages. But it is developing. It is a necessity, because the proletariat wants a full undivided self-consciousness, and poetry is part of this. It is still in its childhood. But even when it grows up the proletariat will not satisfy itself with this poetry alone. It is the legal heir to the whole of past culture, and the heir of all the best things in the poetry of the feudal and bourgeois worlds.

It must acquire this inheritance in such a manner as not to submit to the spirit of the past which reigns in these works — many proletarians have done this before now. The inheritance should not rule the heir, but be a tool in his hands. The dead should serve the living, but not restrain, not chain them.

And for this reason the proletariat must have its *own* poetry. In order not to submit to this alien poetic consciousness strong in its centuries-old maturity the proletariat must acquire its own poetic consciousness, immutable in its clearness. This new consciousness should unfold and enclose the whole of life, the whole of the world, in its creative unity.

Let proletarian poetry then grow and mature, let it help the working class to become what it is destined by history to be — a fighter and destroyer only from external necessity, a creator by all its nature.

Religion, Art and Marxism

There are two great problems for the proletariat to solve in the field of the arts. The first is that of independent creation: the perception of self and of the world in harmonious living images, the expression of its mental forces in artistic forms. The second is that of acquiring its inheritance: it must master the artistic treasures created in the past and assimilate all that is great and beautiful in them, without submitting to the spirit of bourgeois and feudal society reflected in them.

This second problem is not less difficult than the first. We shall inquire into the general methods of its solution.

A religious person who seriously and attentively studies a strange creed exposes himself to the danger of being converted to it, or acquiring from it beliefs which are heresies from the viewpoint of his own religion. Thus it has happened that learned Christians, having devoted themselves to a study of Buddhism, have become Buddhists themselves, or at least have been converted to the moral teaching of Buddhism; the reverse has also happened. The same religious systems may be studied by a freethinker, who sees in all religion only a revelation of the poetic creation of the peoples (this is not the whole truth about religion, but part of it). Is he exposed to the same danger as the religious scholar? Of course not! He may exult in the beauty and depth of the teachings which have attracted hundreds of millions of people, but he perceives them not from the religious but from another and higher viewpoint. The immense richness of thought and feeling which is revealed in Buddhism will certainly appeal to his heart and mind more than to the heart and mind of a learned Christian who cannot get rid of the hidden resistance of his own faith, struggling against the "temptation" of the strange religion; but the fact is that there is no temptation to become a Buddhist for the freethinker – his mind is so constructed as to assimilate the religious material in a manner of its own.

Both the Christian and the freethinker take Buddhism "critically." But the main difference is in the type of their critical attitude, in its bases – "criteria." The believer is not standing above the subject of his study, but approximately on a level with it. He criticises from the standpoint of his own dogma and his own feelings, and he tries to find contradictions in the strange myths and in their moral revaluations; when he discovers such contradictions he is unable to appreciate the poetic or vital truth which is frequently hidden behind them. And even when he penetrates to this truth, he pays for it by a contradiction with himself – he "submits to temptation." He is unable to regard Buddhism as a cultural heritage from a strange world; and if he receives this alien favourably, it conquers him and compels him to become an apostate from his former creed.

The case of the violent atheist is about the same. He is a representative of the progressive, but not sufficiently developed, bourgeois consciousness, who sees in every religion only superstition and deception. He is an "inverted believer." He has risen above religion sufficiently to renounce it, but not enough to understand it. For him religion is also not a heritage; and sometimes it is even a temptation; he comes to feel that it is not only deceit and superstition, but does not understand what it really is.

In quite a different position is our freethinker, representative of the highest stage which may be attained by bourgeois consciousness. His view of religion as a product of the poetical creation of the people allows him, within the limits of this viewpoint, to appreciate his subject quite freely and in an unprejudiced manner. For him it will not present a difficult inner contradiction to learn that the laws of Manu, among the ancient Aryan Hindus, are by the depth of their ideal much more sublime than either ancient or modern Christianity, or that their relation to death, as expressed in their burial rites, is incomparably higher than the Christian in nobleness, sublimity, and beauty. He who is free from all religious consciousness, who will struggle against it whenever it tends to obscure the thought or pervert the will of man, is still in a position to make all religions a valuable cultural heritage for himself and for others.

The attitude of the proletariat to all the culture of the past – of the bourgeois world and of the feudal world – passes through the same stages. In the beginning the worker takes it to be merely culture, culture in general; he does not imagine that culture in its essence can be anything other than that; he is all on a level with it. There may be blunderings in its science and philosophy, there may be false motives in its art, injustices in its morals and laws; but all this is not connected with the essence of it; these are its faults, deviations, imperfections, which further progress would improve.

And though he later on begins to notice in this culture something "bourgeois" and "aristocratic," still he understands these traits only as a defence of the interests of the ruling classes, a "defence" which falsifies the culture; but he still has no doubt as to the essence of this culture, its methods and viewpoint. He is wholly on its level, and while trying to assimilate "whatever is good in it" he is not protected against it even as much as the Buddhist or Brahmin is protected against the temptations of Christianity, or vice versa. He absorbs the old way of thinking and feeling, and the whole attitude towards the world based upon those ways. His own proletarian class viewpoint is preserved only at the moment or the place where he hears sufficiently clearly the imperious voice of class interest speaking. When there is no such clearness and conviction and the problem of life is difficult and complicated, especially when the problem is still new, he does not solve it independently; either a ready-made solution is taken from the surrounding social environment, or even his proletarian class interest is considered and understood from an alien point of view.

Both tendencies have been clearly manifest in the attitude which the working-class intellectuals of the European countries assumed towards the war. Some gave themselves up to the wave

33

of patriotism, almost without stopping even to consider; others were "able to understand" that the "higher interests" of the working class demanded unity with the bourgeoisie to protect or save the fatherland and its wealth, because "their destruction would throw the working class and the whole of civilisation back." This great and cruel experience revealed quite clearly the fact that as long as the proletariat had not worked out its own attitude towards the world, its own way of thinking, its own all-embracing viewpoint, a proletarian cannot master the culture of the past as his inheritance; that culture will master him and use him as human material for its own aims.

If the proletarian, convinced of this, arrives at a mere anarchical negation of the old culture, i.e., if he renounces his heritage, then he puts himself in the position of the naive atheist with his crude attitude towards our religious heritage. But he is in an even worse case, for it is, after all, possible for the bourgeois atheist to do without an understanding of religion – he has other cultural values to depend upon; only the breadth of his thought and the swing of his creation suffer. But the worker is not in a position to put up anything at all to counterpoise the rich and developed culture of the hostile camp; he is unable to create anew anything on a similar scale. It remains a splendid tool or weapon in the hands of his enemies – against him.

The conclusion is obvious. The working class must find and develop to the greatest possible extent a viewpoint that is higher than the culture of the past, just as the viewpoint of the freethinker is the higher in the world of religion. Then it will become possible to master this culture without submitting to it, to turn it into a tool for the construction of a new life, a weapon for the struggle against that same old society from which this culture comes.

Karl Marx made a beginning in the mastery of the mental forces of the old world. The revolution that he accomplished in the field of social science and social philosophy consists in the fact that he revised their basic methods and their results from a new, higher standpoint – which was the proletarian standpoint. Nine-tenths or even more, not only of the materials for his gigantic construction, but also of the methods of their application, were taken by Marx from bourgeois sources; he used the bourgeois classical economists, the reports of the English factory inspectors, the petty bourgeois criticisms of capitalism made by Sismondi and Proudhon, and as a matter of fact all the intellectual Socialism of the Utopians, the dialectics of the German idealists, the materialism of the French Encyclopaedists and of Feyerbach, the social class theories of the French historians and the admirable descriptions of class psychology by Balzac, etc., etc. All this received a new form and was arranged in new combinations, it was turned into a tool for the building of a proletarian organisation, a weapon for the struggle against the rule of capital.

How was this miracle accomplished?

Marx established that society is primarily an organisation for production; this is the basis for all the laws of its life and the development of its forms. This is the standpoint of a socially productive class, it is the standpoint of a toiling collectivity. With this for his starting point, Marx accomplished a criticism of the science of the past, he purified its material, remelted it in the fire of his ideal, and created out of it proletarian knowledge – scientific Socialism.

Thus we see the way in which cultural achievements of the past have been turned into an actual inheritance for the working class: it is by critical rearrangement from the standpoint of collective labour. This is how Marx himself understood his task; it was not by chance that Marx characterised his main work, Capital, as a "Critique of Political Economy."

This is not only true in regard to social science. In all other fields the method of acquiring and assimilating the heritage of the past is by means of our criticism, by proletarian class criticism.

We shall now look more fully into the basis of our criticism. We must find the essence of the standpoint of collective labour.

Three stages may be distinguished in the social process, or, to be more accurate, there are three sides to it: the technical, economic and ideological. On the technical side society struggles against Nature and subjugates it, i.e., it organises the external world in the interests of its life and development. On the economic side – the relations of co-operation and distribution among men – society organises itself for this struggle against Nature. On the ideological side society organises its experience, creating out of this experience the tools for the organisation of its life and development. Consequently, every task in technique, in economics and in the sphere of mental culture is an organisational task, a work of social organisation.

There are and can be no exceptions to this rule. An army may have for its aim destruction, annihilation, disorganisation. But this is not its final aim; the army is itself only a means – a means by which to reorganise the world in the interests of the community to which the army belongs. An artist, an individualist, may imagine that he is creating only for and out of himself; but if he really worked only for himself, his creation would not appeal to anyone beside himself. It would have no relation to mental culture, just as passing and incoherent (but beautiful) dreams are not related to it. And if he tried to create only out of himself, without making any use of the material, the methods of work, creation and expression that he receives from his social environment – then he would not create anything at all.

The standpoint of the labour collectivity is all-organisational. It could not possibly be otherwise with the working class, which organises external matter into products in its labour, organises itself into a creative and fighting community in its co-operation and in its class struggle, and organises its experience into class consciousness by its whole mode of life and by its creative work.

It could not be otherwise, with a class which has to accomplish the historical mission of organising harmoniously the whole life of humanity.

We shall now return to our first illustration. Can and should the whole world of religious creation become a heritage for the working class, against whom every religion has up till now been used as a weapon for enslavement? What use could it find in such an inheritance, what could it do with it?

Our criticism gives a clear and comprehensive reply to this question.

Religion is the solution of an ideological problem for a certain type of community, namely for the authoritarian community. It belongs to the collectivity built upon authoritative collaboration, upon the leading role of some men and the executive role of others, on authority and subordination. Such was the patriarchical clan community, such was feudal society, such were the serf and slave organisations, and such are the bureaucratic police States of to-day; the same state of things prevails in the modern army, and upon a smaller scale in the bourgeois family; and finally capital builds its enterprises on the principle of authority and subordination.

What is the organisational use of a system of accepted ideas? To organise harmoniously the experience of society in such a manner as to suit material organisation, so that cultural achievements may, in their turn, serve society as a means of organisation, to preserve, form, strengthen and further develop the given type of collective organisation. And it is quite easy to perceive how all this is arranged in an authoritarian order of life.

This order is simply transplanted into the field of experience and thought. Every action, whether human or elemental, every phenomenon is represented as a combination of two links – of the organising active will and the passive execution. The whole world is represented as an image of the authoritarian society. At the head of it a supreme authority, a "deity," is put, and, with the complication of the authoritative combinations, a series of subordinated authorities – lower gods, "demigods," "saints," etc., are added, who manage different fields or sides of life. And all these representations are accompanied by authoritarian feelings and moods: admiration, humility, respectful awe. Such are the relationships in religion. It is merely an authoritarian ideology.

It is quite plain what a perfect organisational tool this is for an authoritarian order of life. Religion simply introduces man into this order, assigns to him a definite place in its system, and disciplines him for the execution of the role assigned to him in this system. In feeling, thought and experience the personality is fused with the social environment. It forms an indestructible unit.

The form of religious creation is, for the most part, poetic. This was correctly noted by our freethinker, who did not discern, however, the main thing – the social contents of religion. During those stages of social development when religion is in process of formation, poetry is not yet differentiated from practical and theoretical knowledge, it still includes them in its scope. Religion then includes all and every knowledge, it organises the whole experience of men; knowledge is then understood as a revelation emanating from God, either directly or through some intermediary agents.

What kind of inheritance, then, is religious culture for the proletariat? A very important and valuable one. After it has passed through the worker's criticism it becomes for him a tool not for the support of, but for the understanding of all the authoritarian elements in life. The authoritarian world has decayed, but it is not dead; its vestiges surround us on every side, sometimes openly, but for the most part under the most various and sometimes unexpected disguises. In order to conquer such an enemy, it is necessary to know it, know it thoroughly and seriously.

The question is not only one of renouncing religion; though even in this respect the worker who has acquired the new critical attitude will prove considerably better armed than the furious but naive atheist, who renounces all creeds because of logical calculations, or opposes them with the childish assertion that religion was invented by the priests for the exploitation of the people. More important still is the fact that the possession of this inheritance enables us to form a correct estimate of the significance of the authoritative elements in present-day society, their mutual connection, and their relation to social development. If religion is a tool for the preservation of authoritarian organisation, then it is clear that in the relations of the classes religion for the workers serves only as a means to ensure their subordination, a means to preserve in them the discipline that the ruling classes desire them to possess, in order to keep exploitation secure – in spite of what various religious Socialists say. It is clear that the formula adopted by most Labour parties to the effect that "religion is a private affair" is but a temporary political compromise with which we cannot rest content. It becomes evident why there is such a perpetual alliance between sabre and cassock, between the military and the church; both have a strictly authoritarian organisation. It also becomes clear why the patriarchical petty-bourgeois and peasant family is so attached to religion, to the "law of God"; and at the same time we can see the great danger in the way of social progress that this fecund seed of authoritarianism may represent if it is preserved. A new light is shed upon the role of party leaders, on authorities and the significance of collective control over them.

Further, the whole artistic treasury of the experience of the people, preserved and crystallised as it is in the various holy traditions and letters, pictures of a strange original life with a harmony of its own, is continually broadening the vision of man, giving him a deep insight into the universal motion of humanity, urging him towards new independent creative work which will not be tied down by the usual environment and habits of thought.

Does it, then, not pay the working class to take its religious heritage?

The Workers' Artistic Inheritance

In dealing with religion as an example of the artistic inheritance of the working class I intentionally started out with the most contested and difficult question. In this manner it will be easier for us to master the main problem. It is clear that the weapon with which the working class can and should master that inheritance is that criticism of ours which I have already described, with its new "all-organisational" standpoint of collective labour.

How should our criticism approach its subject?

The soul of a work of art is what we call its "artistic idea." This is its plot and the essence of its treatment, the problem and the principle of its solution. Of what kind, then, is this problem? We know now. No matter how it has been considered by the artist himself, in reality it is always a problem of organisation. It is this in two senses: in the first it is a question of how to organise harmoniously a certain sum total of the elements of life and experience; in the second sense, it is a question of how to ensure that the unity created in this way may serve as a means of organisation for a certain community. If the first is not accomplished we have no art, but only confusion; if the second is not accomplished, then the work has no interest for anybody except the author himself, and is of no use whatever.

We shall take for an illustration one of the greatest works of world-literature, the finest diamond of the old cultural heritage – Shakespeare's *Hamlet*.

What is the "artistic idea" of this work? It is the organisational problem of a human soul torn by the difficult contradictions of life, divided between the striving towards happiness, love and harmony, and the necessity of waging a painful, stern, merciless struggle. Where is the way out of this contradiction, how can all this be reconciled? How can the thirst

41

for harmony be prevented from weakening a man in the inevitable struggle of life, be prevented from robbing him of the strength, firmness and coolness which are necessary for this struggle? At the same time, how can a man avoid the involuntary cruelty of the blows, the blood and dirt of the wounds, destroying the whole joy, the whole beauty of existence? What should be done to restore harmony to the soul rent asunder by the sharp conflict between its deepest and sublimest need, and the imperious demand dictated by the hostility of his environment?

We perceive at once how vast is the scale of this organisational problem, how great is its significance for every man. It is not a problem which faces the Danish Prince alone, nor the numerous "Hamlets" and "little Hamlets" of our middle class and its literature. This problem is an inevitable moment in the life of every man; he who is strong enough to solve it is raised by it to a higher stage of self-consciousness; for the man who cannot solve the problem becomes a source of spiritual ruin, and sometimes even leads to his destruction.

This tragedy penetrates perhaps most acutely the soul of the proletarian idealist, and even more so the collective psychology of the working class. Fraternity is its ideal, the harmonious life of humanity is its highest aim; but how removed from all this is its surrounding environment, how difficult and at times gloomy and cruel is the struggle forced upon it! Yet it must fight if it does not want to be deprived of all that has been attained by previous innumerable exertions, if it does not want to lose its social dignity and the very sense of life. Little joys have been given it, and great is the thirst for them; but even that little is constantly threatened with destruction or deformation by the inevitable elements of social hatred and anarchy. Why, the very ability to love and rejoice may be killed in the exasperation of the fight, in the despair of defeats and in the rage of the countering blows!

The tragedy of Hamlet enfolds itself on just such a basis. He is a very gifted man, with a fine artistic nature; and at the same time life has favoured him. His education as a prince and heir to the throne, several years of wandering in Germany in the capacity of a student, the fullest enjoyment afforded by occupation in the sciences and arts, life in an environment of friendship and good cheer: finally his serene poetical love for Ophelia – it is seldom that a man has an existence so happy and harmonious. Hamlet takes it as a matter of course. He has never experienced, nor can he imagine, any other existence. But then the time comes, the horror and hideousness of life breaks in upon him – at first in dark foreboding and then with painful clearness.

His family has been destroyed, the lawful order of his country has been shattered to the ground. A traitor and fratricide has seized the throne of his father and seduced his mother; at the court, hypocrisy, intrigue and licentiousness are reigning; decline of the old good customs is spreading over the country, breeding confusion. It is necessary to restore law, to cut short crime, to avenge the death of his father and the disgrace of his family. Such is the sacred duty of Hamlet, as defined by the whole order of his feudal conceptions.

Is he sufficiently strong to accomplish all this? Yes, in his rich nature there are the requisite powers. For he is not only an artist and a favourite of fortune, he is not only a "passive aesthetic" for whose life harmony is as indispensable as air. He is, besides, the son of a warrior king, a descendant of the great Vikings; he has received a perfect military education. There is a fighter in him – but one that has not had the opportunity to unfold, to put himself to the test; and, what is worse, the fighter is combined with the, passive aesthete.

Here is the essence of the tragedy. The struggle demands from Hamlet resort to cunning, deception, violence and cruelty; but these are repulsive to his mild and refined soul. And more, he has to direct them against his nearest and dearest: in the camp of his enemies he finds his beloved mother, and he sees that Ophelia herself is used as a tool in the intrigues against him. His enemies put them forward, and thus play skilfully upon the weakest sides of his soul. His hand, which is raised for the blow, is stopped; the inner struggle paralyses his will, the momentary resolution gives way to hesitation and inaction, time passes in fruitless meditation – the result is a deep duality and for a time even the wreck of his personality: everything is confused in the chaos of unavoidable contradictions, Hamlet "becomes insane."

An ordinary person would have been crushed by the circumstances and would have perished before he could do anything. But Hamlet is a figure not of the ordinary. He is an heroic character. Through the tortures of despair, through the sickness of his soul, he still goes step by step to the real solution. The elements of the two separated personalities in one – of the aesthete and the warrior – penetrate each other and are welded in a new personality: the active aesthete, the champion of the harmony of life. The main contradiction disappears: the thirst for harmony finds an outlet in the exertion of fighting, the blood and mire of the struggle are directly redeemed by the consciousness that it serves to purify life and raise it to a higher level. The organisational problem is solved, the artistic idea has been clothed in form.

Hamlet, it is true, perished; and in this the great poet is objectively right, as always. The enemies of Hamlet had this advantage: while he was gathering the forces of his soul, they acted, and prepared everything for his destruction. But he dies a victor: crime is punished, the lawful order is restored, the fate of Denmark is entrusted to firm hands: to the young hero Fortinbras. He is not so great a man as Hamlet, but has an harmonious character imbued with the principles of the feudal world, whose ideals inspired Hamlet also.

Here another aspect of our criticism comes in. The organisational problem has been solved; but which collectivity was it that gave the author the vital material for the embodiment of this problem? Of course, it was not the proletarian, which did not exist then. The author of Hamlet, no matter who he was – as is well known this is a disputed question – was either an aristocrat himself or a fervent adherent of the aristocracy. It is from this world that he draws the greater part of the material for his dramas, and his works bear the seal of the feudal monarchical ideal. The bases of that social order are authority and subordination, faith in a deity managing the world, faith in the holiness and infallibility of the order which has been established since ancient times, and the recognition that some people are higher beings, by their very birth destined to manage and rule, while others are lower and must be ruled, being incapable of, any other function but that of subordination. Now, does not all this destroy the value of the work for the working class?

I shall answer by another question. Is it necessary for the working class to know other organisational types besides its own? Moreover, is the working class in general able to work out and form its own type otherwise than by way of comparison with others, by the criticism of others, by working them over and using their elements? And who else, if not the great and skilful artist, can lead one into the very depths of an alien organisation of life and thought? It is the task of our criticism to expose the historical significance of that organisation, its connection with lower stages of development, its contradiction with the vital conditions and problems of the proletariat. As soon as this is accomplished there is no more danger of submitting to the influence of the strange type of organisation; the knowledge of it becomes one of our most precious tools for the creation of our own organisation.

And here also the objectivity of the great artist affords the best support for our criticism. Without making it his aim he happens to delineate all the conservatism of the authoritarian world, its inherent narrowness, and the weakness of the human mind in this world. It is worth while to recollect the appearance of the hero Fortinbras, which serves as an impulse towards a change in the soul of Hamlet himself, urging him to enter the course of action leading to the solution of his problem. With a proud conviction of his own right, without any doubts or hesitation, Fortinbras leads his army to conquer a stretch of land which is not worth, perhaps, the blood of one of the soldiers who will perish in this war. . . .

Finally, great significance attaches to the fact that while the organisational problem is set before us and solved on the basis of the life of a society strange to us, while the solution in its general aspect preserves its validity for the present time, and for the proletariat as a class also, whenever the thirst for harmony clashes with the severe demands of its struggle. Here art teaches the working class the universal setting and the universal solution of organisational problems – which is necessary for it in the accomplishment of its universal organisational ideal.

The Belgian artist, Constantine Meunier, in his sculptures depicted the life of the workers. His statue, "The Philosopher," represents a worker thinking, deeply absorbed in the solution of some important philosophical problem. The naked figure makes an integral and strong impression of exerted thought, concentrated on one thing, and overcoming some great invisible resistance.

What is the artistic idea of the statue? The organisational problem is the following: How to combine hard, physical labour with the strain of thought, with mental creative work? The solution of the problem . . .?

It is only necessary to look at the figure of "The Philosopher," which is penetrated throughout by reserved effort, in which every visible muscle is fully exerted – an exertion not manifesting itself in any external action, but seeming to pass into the inner depths – and immediately the solution comes forward with the greatest vividness and impressiveness. It is this: "Thought is a physical exertion in itself; its nature is the same as that of labour, there is no contradiction between them, their division is artificial and passing." The results of exact science, of physiological psychology, confirm this idea; but it is more intimate and comprehensible in its artistic expression. And its enormous significance for the proletariat does not need proof.

But our criticism must put the question: On the standpoint of which class or social group does the artist stand in his creative work? And then it will become plain that although he represents workers, he does it not as an ideologist of the working class: his is the standpoint of labour, but not of collective labour. The worker-thinker is taken as an individual; those connections which fuse the exertion of his thought with the physical and mental exertions of millions, making it a link in the universal chain of labour, are not felt at all, or at best are delineated very vaguely, almost indiscernibly. The artist is an intellectual by his social position; he is accustomed to work individually himself, without noticing to what extent his labour is connected with the collective labour of humanity both by its origin and by its methods and problems. In this the standpoint of the toiling intellectuals is very little different from that of the bourgeoisie – it is just as individualistic – and here also our criticism must supplement that which the artist could not give.

Thus the tasks of proletarian criticism in relation to the art of the past define themselves. By carrying out these tasks it will give the working class an opportunity to master firmly and use independently the organisational experience of thousands of years crystallised in artistic forms.

The usual conception of the role and sense of proletarian criticism is different. It most frequently defends the position of "social arts," and deals with the problems of its agitational significance in defence of the interest of the working class. Some years ago the worker Ivan Kubikov invited the proletarians to study the best works of the literature of the old world, regarding art's educational influence in the following manner. No doubt there is in this literature "not only pure gold, but also elements of alloy which are harmful for the proletariat." These elements are the "conservative moderating forces." But they are not to be feared, because the worker has his class sense which allows him to distinguish between the gold and the alloy. "If we observe attentively the impressions received from art we shall find that only the gold affects, the alloy passes by the consciousness of the worker. . . . I have personally had the opportunity during my observations to see the very surprising way in which a rebel worker manages to draw revolutionary conclusions from the most innocent works of art." ("Nasha Zaria," *Our Dawn*, 1914, No. 3, pp. 48-49). This is a naive standpoint, and faulty at its base.

There is very little good in such a sense which "manages" to draw revolutionary conclusions from a really innocent work. Misrepresentation is misrepresentation. What does it prove? That there is a great force of direct feeling and a lack of objectivity. It proves that the thought is lower than this feeling and submits to it. Should that be the consciousness of a class destined to solve the universal organisational problem?

As an illustration of the interrelation between "gold and alloy" Kubikov takes Schiller's *Don Karlos*; he thinks that the detection of tyranny and the fiery orations of Marquis Posa are the gold, while his dreams about monarchy absolute, but enlightened and humane, is the alloy. This is not true. On "fiery words," accompanied by vagueness and weakness of thought, the reader might well be brought up in the direction of revolutionary phraseology alone. On the contrary, the live and deeply artistic expression of the ideal of enlightened monarchy is not at all "alloy" for the historically conscious reader who has the standpoint of proletarian criticism. The ideal is the mental model of organisation; the knowledge and understanding of such models which have been worked out by the past is indispensable for a class which is called upon to organise the future. In the struggle of the heroic personalities presented by the artist it is necessary to discern the struggle of social forces which have defined and determined the thought and will of the men of that epoch, and the necessity of the different ideals called forth by the nature of those forces. To get an artistic insight into the soul of perished classes or of those which are passing from history, as well as into the soul of the classes which occupy the scene of history at present, is one of the best means to master the accumulated cultural and organisational experience of man, the most precious inheritance for a class that comes to construct.

And as far as the art of the past can educate the feelings and moods of the proletariat, it should serve as a means to deepen and enlighten them, to extend their field over all the life of humanity, along all its path of toil, but it should not serve as a means of agitation, a tool for propaganda.

The critic who manages to present to the proletariat a great work of the old culture, in the theatre for instance, after the performance of a piece of genius, who can explain to the spectators its sense and value from the organisational standpoint of collective labour, or give them such an explanation in a short and comprehensible programme, or perhaps can explain in an article in a Labour newspaper or magazine the poem or novel of a great master – such a critic will accomplish a serious and important work for the proletariat.

Here is our broadest field for work, for work which will be important and lasting.

Appendix: Class and Art (Speech by Leon Trotsky)

Speech delivered May 9, 1924 during discussion at the Press Department of the Central Committee of the RCP(B) on Party Policy in the Field of Imaginative Literature.

Trotsky: It seems to me that it is Comrade Raskolnikov who has given most distinctive expression here to the point of view of the **Na Postu** group – you can't get away from that, comrades of the *Na Postu* group! After a long absence, Raskolnikov spoke here with all the freshness of Afghanistan, whereas the other **Na Postu** people, having tasted a little of the tree of knowledge, tried to cover their nakedness – except Comrade Vardin, however, who goes on living the way he was born. (**Vardin:** *"Why, you didn't hear what I said here!"*) True, I arrived late. But, first, I read your article in the last issue of **Na Postu**; secondly, I have just glanced through the verbatim record of your speech; and, thirdly, it must be said that one can tell beforehand, without listening to you, what you are going to say. (*Laughter*)

But to return to Comrade Raskolnikov. He says: they recommend the "fellow-travellers" to us, but did the old, pre-war **Pravda** or **Zvezda** print the words of Artsybashev, Leonid Andreyev and others whom now they would certainly call "fellow-travellers"? There is an example of a fresh approach to the question, not spoilt by any reflections. What are Artsybashev and Andreyev doing here? So far as I know, nobody has called them "fellow-travellers". Leonid Andreyev died in a state of epileptic hatred of soviet Russia. Artsybashev was not so long ago simply pushed over the frontier. One can't muddle things up in such a shameless way! What is a "fellow-traveller"? In literature as in politics we call by this name someone who, stumbling and staggering, goes up to a certain point along the same road which we shall follow much further. Whoever goes *against* us is not a fellow-traveller but an enemy, whom if necessary we will deport, for the well-being of the revolution is our highest law. How can you mix up Leonid Andreyev in this question of "fellow-travellers"? (**Raskolnikov:** *"Well, but what about Pilnyak?"*) If you are going to talk about Artsybashev when you mean Pilnyak, there's no arguing with you. (*Laughter. A shout:* *"But aren't they the same thing?"*) What do you mean: aren't they the same thing? If you name names, you must stick to them. Pilnyak may be good or bad, in this way or that he may be good or he may be bad – but Pilnyak is Pilnyak, and you must talk about him as Pilnyak, and not as Leonid Andreyev. Knowledge in general begins with distinguishing between things and appearances, and not with chaotic confusion . Raskolnikov says: "We didn't invite 'fellow-travellers' into the pages of **Zvezda** and **Pravda**, but sought and found poets and writers in the depths of the proletariat." Sought and found! In the depths of the proletariat! But what did you do with them? Why have you hidden them from us? (**Raskolnikov:** *"There is, for instance, Demyan Bedny."*) Oh, well now, that I didn't know, I must confess – that we discovered Demyan Bedny in the depths of the proletariat. (*General laughter*) You see with what methods we are approaching the problem of literature: we speak of Leonid Andreyev, and we mean Pilnyak, we boast that we have found writers and poets in the depths of the proletariat, and then when we call the roll, out of these "depths" there answers only Demyan Bedny. (*Laughter*) This won't do. This is frivolity. Much more seriousness is needed in considering this matter.

Let us try, indeed, to look more seriously at those pre-revolutionary workers' publications, newspapers and periodicals, which have been mentioned here. We all remember that they used to carry some verses devoted to the struggle, to May Day, and so on. All these verses, such as they were, constituted very important and significant documents in the history of culture. They expressed the revolutionary awakening and political growth of the working class. In this cultural-historical sense their importance was no less than that of the works of all the Shakespeares, Molières and Pushkins in the world. In these feeble verses was the pledge of a new and higher human culture which the awakened masses will create when they have mastered the elements of the old culture. But, all the same, the workers' verses in **Zvezda** and **Pravda** do not at all signify the rise of a new, proletarian literature. Inartistic doggerel in the Derzhavin (or pre-Derzhavin) style cannot be regarded as a new literature, although those thoughts and feelings which sought expression in these verses also belong to a writer who is beginning to appear from the working-class milieu. It is wrong to suppose that the development of literature is an unbroken chain, in which the naïve, though sincere, doggerel of young workers at the beginning of this century is the first link in the coming "proletarian literature". In reality, these revolutionary verses were a political event, not a literary one. They contributed not to the growth of literature but to the growth of the revolution. The revolution led to the victory of the proletariat, the victory of the proletariat is leading to the transformation of the economy. The transformation of the economy is in process of changing the cultural state of the working masses. And the cultural growth of the working people will create the real basis for a new art. "But it is impossible to permit duality," Comrade Raskolnikov tells us. "It is necessary that in our publications political writing and poetry should form one whole; Bolshevism is distinguished by monolithicity," and so on. At first sight this reasoning seems irrefutable. Actually, it is an empty abstraction. At best it is a pious but unreal wish for something good. Of course it would be splendid if we had, to supplement our Communist political writing, the Bolshevik world-outlook expressed in artistic form. But we haven't, and that is not accidental. The heart of the matter is that artistic creativity, by its very nature, lags behind the other modes of expression of a man's spirit, and still more of the spirit of a class. It is one thing to understand something and express it logically, and quite another thing to assimilate it organically,

53

reconstructing the whole system of one's feelings, and to find a new kind of artistic expression for this new entity. The latter process is more organic, slower, more difficult to subject to conscious influence – and in the end it will always lag behind. The political writing of a class hastens ahead on stilts, while its artistic creativity hobbles along behind on crutches. Marx and Engels were great political writers of the proletariat in the period when the class was still not really awakened. (**From the meeting:** *"Yes, you're right there."*) I am very grateful to you. (*Laughter*) But take the trouble to draw the necessary conclusions from this, and understand why there is not this monolithicity between political writing and poetry, and this will in turn help you to understand why in the old legal Marxist periodicals we always found ourselves in a bloc, or semi-bloc, with artistic "fellow-travellers", sometimes very dubious and even plainly false ones. You remember, of course, **Novoye Slovo**, the best of the old legal Marxist periodicals, in which many Marxists of the older generation collaborated including Vladimir Ilyich. This periodical, as everyone knows, was friendly with the Decadents. What was the reason for that? It was because the Decadents were then a young and persecuted tendency in bourgeois literature. And this persecuted situation of theirs impelled them to take sides with our attitude of opposition, though the latter, of course, was quite different in character, in spite of which the Decadents were temporarily fellow-travellers with us. And later Marxist periodicals (and the semi-Marxist ones, it goes without saying), right down to **Prosveshcheniye**, had no sort of "monolithic" fiction section, but set aside considerable space for the "fellow-travellers". Some might be either more severe or more indulgent in this respect, but it was impossible to carry on a "monolithic" policy in the field of art, because the artistic elements needed for such a policy were lacking.

But Raskolnikov at bottom doesn't want this. In works of art he ignores that which makes them works of art. This was most vividly shown in his remarkable judgement on Dante's *Divine*

Comedy, which in his opinion is valuable to us just because it enables us to understand the psychology of a certain class at a certain time. To put the matter that way means simply to strike out the *Divine Comedy* – from the realm of art. Perhaps the time has come to do that, but if so we must understand the essence of the question and not shrink from the conclusions. If I say that the importance of the *Divine Comedy* lies in the fact that it gives me an understanding of the state of mind of certain classes in a certain epoch, this means that I transform it into a mere historical document, for, as a work of art, the *Divine Comedy* must speak in some way to my feelings and moods. Dante's work may act on me in a depressing way, fostering pessimism and despondency in me, or, on the contrary, it may rouse, inspire, encourage me. This is the fundamental relationship between a reader and a work of art. Nobody, of course, forbids a reader to assume the role of a researcher and approach the *Divine Comedy* as merely an historical document. It is clear, though, that these two approaches are on two different levels, which, though connected, do not overlap. How is it thinkable that there should be not an historical but a directly aesthetic relationship between us and a medieval Italian book? This is explained by the fact that in class society, in spite of all its changeability, there are certain common features. Works of art developed in a medieval Italian city can, we find, affect us too. What does this require? A small thing: it requires that these feelings and moods shall have received such broad, intense, powerful expression as to have raised them above the limitations of the life of those days. Dante was, of course, the product of a certain social milieu. But Dante was a genius. He raised the experience of his epoch to a tremendous artistic height. And if we, while today approaching other works of medieval literature merely as objects of study, approach the *Divine Comedy* as a source of artistic perception, this happens not because Dante was a Florentine petty bourgeois of the 13th century but, to a considerable extent, in spite of that circumstance. Let us take, for instance, such an elementary psychological feeling as fear of death. This feeling is characteristic not only of man but also of animals. In man it first found simple articulate expression, and later also artistic expression. In different ages, in different social milieux, this expression has changed, that is to say, men have feared death in different ways. And nevertheless what was said on this score not only by Shakespeare, Byron, Goethe, but also by the Psalmist, can move us. (*Exclamation by Comrade Libedinsky*) Yes, yes, I came in at the very moment when you, Comrade Libedinsky, were explaining to Comrade Voronsky in the terms of elementary political instruction (you yourself put it like that) about the variation in feelings and states of mind in different classes. In that general form it is indisputable. However, for all that, you won't deny that Shakespeare and Byron somehow speak to your soul and mine. (**Libedinsky:** *"They will soon stop speaking."*) Whether it will be soon, I don't know, but undoubtedly a time will come when people will approach the works of Shakespeare and Byron in the same way as we approach most poets of the Middle Ages, that is, exclusively from the standpoint of scientific-historical analysis. Even sooner, however, will come the time when people will stop seeking in Marx's **Capital** for precepts for their practical activity, and **Capital** will have become merely an historical document, together with the program of our party. But at present we do not yet intend to put Shakespeare, Byron, Pushkin in the archives, and we will continue to recommend them to the workers. Comrade Sosnovsky, for instance, strongly recommends Pushkin, declaring that he will undoubtedly last another fifty years. Let us not speak of periods of time. But in what sense can we recommend Pushkin to a worker? There is no proletarian class viewpoint in Pushkin, not to speak of a monolithic expression of Communist feelings. Of course, Pushkin's language is magnificent – that cannot be denied – but, after all, this language is used by him for expressing the world-outlook of the nobility. Shall we say to the worker: read Pushkin in order to understand how a nobleman, a serf-owner and gentleman of the bed chamber, encountered Spring and experienced Autumn? This element is, of course, present in

Pushkin, for Pushkin grew up on a particular social basis. But the expression that Pushkin gave his feelings is so saturated with the artistic, and generally with the psychological, experience of centuries, is so crystallized, that it has lasted down to our times and, according to Comrade Sosnovsky, will last another fifty years. And when people tell me that the artistic significance of Dante for us consists in his expressing the way of life of a certain epoch, that only makes one spread one's hands in helplessness. I am sure that many, like me, would, after reading Dante, have to strain their memories to remember the date and place of his birth, and yet none the less, this would not have prevented us from getting artistic delight, if not from the whole of the *Divine Comedy* then at least from some parts of it. Since I am not a historian of the Middle Ages, my attitude to Dante is predominantly artistic. (**Ryazanov:** *"That's an exaggeration. 'To read Dante is to take a bath in the sea', said Shevyryev, who was also against history, replying to Byelinsky."*) I don't doubt that Shevyryev did express himself as Comrade Ryazanov says, but I am not against history – that's pointless. Of course the historical approach to Dante is legitimate and necessary and affects our aesthetic attitude to him, but one can't substitute one for the other. I remember what Kareyev wrote on this point, in a polemic with the Marxists: let them, the Marxides (that was how they ironically spoke of the Marxists in those days) tell us, for instance, what class interests dictated the *Divine Comedy*. And from the other side, the Italian Marxist, old Antonio Labriola, wrote something like this: "Only fools could try to interpret the text of the *Divine Comedy* as though it were made of the cloth that Florentine merchants provided for their customers." I remember this expression almost word for word because in the polemic with the subjectivists I had occasion to quote these words more than once, in the old days. I think that Comrade Raskolnikov's attitude not only to Dante but to art in general proceeds not from the Marxist criterion but from that of the late Shulyatikov, who provided a caricature of Marxism in this connection. Antonio Labriola also made his vigorous comment

57

on this sort of caricature.

"By proletarian literature I understand literature which looks at the world with the eyes of the vanguard," and so on, and so on. This is the opinion of Comrade Lelevich. Splendid, we are ready to accept his definition. Give us though, not only the definition but, also the literature. Where is it? Show us it! (**Lelevich:** *"Komsomolia – there is the best of recent times."*) What times? (**A voice:** *"The last year."*) Well, all right, the last year. I don't want to speak polemically. My attitude to Bezymensky has nothing in it that can be called negative, I hope. I praised **Komsomolia** highly when I read it in manuscript. But regardless of whether we can on this account proclaim the appearance of proletarian literature, I can say that Bezymensky would not exist as an artist if we did not have Mayakovsky, Pasternak and even Pilnyak. (**A voice:** *"That proves nothing."*) This does prove, at least, – that the artistic creativity of a given epoch is a very complex web which is not woven automatically, by discussion groups and seminars, but comes into being through complex interrelations, in the first place with the different fellow-travelling groups. You can't get away from that; Bezymensky doesn't try to, and he does well not to. In some of his works, the influence of "fellow-travellers" is even too noticeable. But this is an unavoidable phenomenon of youth and growth. And here we have Comrade Libedinsky, the enemy of "fellow-travellers", and himself an imitator of Pilnyak and even Byely. Yes, yes, Comrade Averbach must excuse me; I see him shaking his head, though without, much conviction. Libedinsky's last story, *Zavtra* [*Tomorrow*] is like the diagonal of a parallelogram, one side of which is Pilnyak and the other Andrei Byely. In itself that's no misfortune – Libedinsky can't be born in the land of **Na Postu** as a ready-made writer. (**Voice:** *"It's a very barren land."*) I have already spoken about Libedinsky, after the first appearance of his **Nedelya [The Week]**. Bukharin then, as you will recall, fervently praised it, out of the expansiveness and kindness of his nature, and this praise alarmed me. Meanwhile I was obliged to observe the extreme dependence of Comrade Libedinsky on those very writers – "fellow-travellers" and semi-fellow-travellers – whom he and his co-thinkers all curse in **Na Postu**. You see once more that art and political writing are not always monolithic. I have no intention of giving up Comrade Libedinsky as a bad job on that account. I think that it is clear to all of us that our common duty is to show the greatest concern for every young artistic talent ideologically close to us, and all the more when it is a matter of someone who is our brother-in-arms. The first condition of such an attentive and considerate attitude is not to give premature praise, killing the young writer's self-criticism; the second condition is not to wash one's hands of the man at once if he stumbles. Comrade Libedinsky is still very young. He needs to learn and to grow. And in this connection it turns out that Pilnyak fulfils a need. (**A voice:** *"For Libedinsky or for us?"*) First of all, for Libedinsky. (**Libedinsky:** *"But this means that I've been poisoned by Pilnyak."*) Alas, the human organism can be nourished only by taking poison and producing internal resources that combat the poison. That's life. If you let yourself go dry, like a Caspian roach, that won't mean you're poisoned, but you won't be nourished either; indeed, it will mean nothing at all will happen. (*Laughter*)

Comrade Pletnev, speaking here in defence of his abstractions about proletarian culture and its constituent part, proletarian literature, quoted Vladimir Ilyich against me. Now there's something that's really to the point! We must give that proper consideration. Not long ago an entire booklet appeared, written by Pletnev, Tretiakov and Sizov, in which proletarian literature was defended by means of quotations from Lenin against Trotsky. This method is very fashionable nowadays. Vardin could write a whole thesis on the subject. But the fact is, Comrade Pletnev, that you know very well how matters stood, because you yourself appealed to me to save you from the thunders of Vladimir Ilyich, who was going, you thought, on account of this very "proletarian culture" of yours, to close down

Proletkult altogether. And I promised you that I would defend the continued existence of *Proletkult*, on certain grounds, but that as regards Bogdanov's abstractions about proletarian culture I was entirely opposed to you and your protector Bukharin, and entirely in agreement with Vladimir Ilyich.

Comrade Vardin, who speaks here as nothing less than the living embodiment of Party tradition, does not shrink from trampling in the crudest way on what Lenin wrote about proletarian culture. As we know, there is plenty of empty piety around: people "firmly agree" with Lenin and then preach the absolute opposite to his views. In terms that leave room for no other interpretation, Lenin mercilessly condemned "chatter about proletarian culture". However, there is nothing simpler than getting away from this evidence: why, of course, Lenin condemned chatter about proletarian culture, but, don't you see, it was only chatter that he condemned, and we are not chattering but seriously getting down to work, and even standing with our arms akimbo. They only forget that Lenin's sharp condemnation was aimed precisely at those who are now referring to him. Empty piety, I repeat, is available in plenty: refer to Lenin and do the contrary.

The comrades who have spoken here under the sign of proletarian culture approach different ideas according to the attitude of the authors of those ideas to their *Proletkult* groups. I have tested this and found it true as regards my own fate. My book on literature, which caused so much alarm among certain comrades, appeared originally, as some of you may perhaps recall, in the form of articles in **Pravda**. I wrote this book over a period of two years, during two summer breaks. This circumstance, as we see today, is of importance in relation to the question that interests us. When it appeared, in the form of newspaper articles, the first part of the book, dealing with "non-October" literature, with the "fellow-travellers", with the "peasant-singers", and exposing the limitedness and contradictions of the ideological-artistic position of the fellow-travellers, the **Na Postu** comrades hailed me with enthusiasm – everywhere you cared to look you found quotations from my articles on the fellow-travellers. At one stage I was quite depressed by it. (*Laughter*) My estimation of the "fellow-travellers", I repeat, was regarded as practically faultless; even Vardin made no objections to it. (**Vardin:** *"And I don't object to it now."*) That is just what I say. But why then do you now obliquely and insinuatingly argue against me about the "fellow-travellers"? What is going on here? At first sight it's quite incomprehensible. But the solution is a simple one: my crime is not that I incorrectly defined the social nature of the fellow-travellers or their artistic significance – no, Comrade Vardin even now, as we heard, "does not object" to that – my crime is that I did not bow before the manifestos of **Oktyabr** or **Kuznitsa**, that I did not acknowledge these groups as the monopolist representatives of the artistic interests of the proletariat – in short, that I did not identify the cultural-historical interests and tasks of the class with the intentions, plans and pretensions of certain literary groups. That was where I went wrong. And when this became clear, then there arose the howl, unexpected by its belatedness: Trotsky is on the side of the petty-bourgeois "fellow-traveller"! Am I for the "fellow-travellers", or against them? In what sense am I against them? You knew that nearly two years ago, from my articles on the "fellow-travellers". But then you agreed, you praised, you quoted, you gave your approval. And when, a year later, it turned out that my criticism of the "fellow-travellers" was not at all just an approach to the glorification of some amateurish literary group or other, then the writers and defenders of this group, or rather of these groups, began to bring forward philosophical arguments against my allegedly incorrect attitude to the "fellow-travellers". Oh, strategists! My offence was not that I estimated incorrectly Pilnyak or Mayakovsky – the **Na Postu** group added nothing to what I had said, but merely repeated it in vulgarized form – my offence was that I knocked their own literary factory! In the whole of their peevish criticism there is not the shadow of a class approach. What we find is the attitude of one literary group engaged in competition with others, and that's all.

I mentioned the "peasant-singers", and we have heard here that the **Na Postu** group especially approved of that chapter. It's not enough to approve, you should understand. What is the point here regarding the "peasant-singing" fellow-travellers? It is that this is a phenomenon which is not accidental, is not of minor importance and is not ephemeral. In our country, please don't forget, we have the dictatorship of the proletariat in a country which is inhabited mainly by peasants. The intelligentsia is placed between these two classes as between two millstones, is ground up little by little and arises anew, and cannot be ground up completely, that is, it will remain as an "intelligentsia" for a long time yet, until the full development of socialism and a very considerable rise in the cultural level of the entire population of the country. The intelligentsia serves the workers' and peasants' state and subordinates itself to the proletariat, partly from fear, partly from conviction; it wavers and will continue to waver in accordance with the course of events, and it will seek ideological support for its waverings in the peasantry – this is the source of the Soviet literature of the "peasant-singers". What are the prospects of this school? Is it basically hostile to us? Does its path lead towards us or away to us? And this depends on the general course of events. The task of the proletariat consists in retaining all-round hegemony over the peasantry and leading it to socialism. If we were to suffer a setback on this road, that is, if there were to be a break between the proletariat and the peasantry, then the "peasant-singing" intelligentsia, or, more correctly, 99 per cent of the entire intelligentsia, would turn against the proletariat. But this eventuality is not at all inevitable. We are, on the contrary, following a course aimed at bringing the peasantry, under the leadership of the proletariat, to socialism. This is a very, very long road. In the course of this process both the proletariat and the peasantry will bring forward their own intelligentsia. It need not be supposed that the intelligentsia

62

arising from the proletariat will be a 100 per cent proletarian intelligentsia. The very fact that the proletariat is obliged to promote from its ranks a special stratum of "cultural workers" inevitably means a more or less considerable cultural disconnection between the remainder of the class as a whole and the proletarians promoted from it. This applies even more in the case of the peasant intelligentsia. The peasants' road to socialism is not at all the same as the proletariat's. And in so far as the intelligentsia, even an arch-Soviet intelligentsia, is unable to merge its road with the road of the proletarian vanguard, to that degree it tries to find a political, ideological, artistic support for itself in the peasant, whether real or imagined. This appears all the more in the sphere of fiction, where we have an old Populist tradition. Is this for us or against us? I repeat: the answer entirely depends on the entire future course of development. If we draw the peasant, towed by the proletariat, to socialism – and we confidently believe that we shall draw him – then the creative work of the "peasant-singers" will evolve by complex and tortuous paths into the socialist art of the future. This complexity of the problems involved, and at the same time their reality and concreteness, is completely beyond the understanding of the **Na Postu** group, and not only of them. This is their fundamental mistake. Talking about the "fellow-travellers" regardless of this social basis and prospect means simply wagging one's tongue.

Allow me, comrades, to say a little more about Comrade Vardin's tactics in the field of literature, in relation to his last article in **Na Postu**. In my view this is not tactics but a disgrace! An amazingly supercilious tone, but deadly little knowledge or understanding. No understanding of art as art, that is, as a particular, specific field of human creativity; nor any Marxist understanding of the conditions and ways of development of art. Instead, an unworthy juggling of quotations from White-Guard publications abroad which, do you see, have praised Comrade Voronsky for publishing the works of Pilnyak, or ought to have praised him, or said something against Vardin and, maybe, for

Voronsky, and so on, and so on – in that spirit of "circumstantial evidence" which has to make up for the lack of knowledge and understanding. Comrade Vardin's last article is built on the idea that a White-Guard newspaper supported Voronsky against Vardin, writing that the whole conflict came down to the point that Voronsky approached literature from the literary point of view. "Comrade Voronsky, by his political behaviour," says Vardin, "has fully deserved this White-Guard kiss." But this is an insinuation, not an analysis of the question! If Vardin disagrees with the multiplication table, while Voronsky finds himself in this matter on the same side as a White Guard who knows arithmetic, Voronsky's political reputation has nothing to fear from that. Yes, art has to be approached as art, literature as literature, that is, as a quite specific field of human endeavour. Of course we have a class criterion in art too, but this class criterion must be refracted artistically, that is, in conformity with the quite specific peculiarities of that field of creativity to which we are applying our criterion. The bourgeoisie knows this very well, it likewise approaches art from its class point of view, it knows how to get from art what it needs, but only because it approaches art as art. What is there to wonder at if an artistically-literate bourgeois has a disrespectful attitude to Vardin, who approaches art from the standpoint of political "circumstantial evidence", and not with a class-artistic criterion? And if there is anything that makes me feel ashamed it is not that in this dispute I may find myself formally in the same boat with some White Guard who understands art, but that, before the eyes of this White Guard I am obliged to explain the first letters in the alphabet of art to a Party publicist who writes articles about art. What a cheapening of Marxism this is: instead of making a Marxist analysis of the question, one finds a quotation from **Rul** or **Dyen** and around it piles up abuse and insinuations!

One cannot approach art as one can politics, not because artistic creation is a religious rite or something mystical, as somebody here ironically said, but because it has its own laws of development, and above all because in artistic creation an enormous role is played by subconscious processes – slower, more idle and less subjected to management and guidance, just because they are subconscious. It has been said here that those writings of Pilnyak's which are closer to Communism are feebler than those which are politically further away from us. What is the explanation? Why, just this, that on the rationalistic plane Pilnyak is ahead of himself as an artist. To consciously swing himself round on his own axis even only a few degrees is a very difficult task for an artist, often connected with a profound, sometimes fatal crisis. And what we are considering is not an individual or group change in creative endeavour, but such a change on the class, social scale. This is a long and very complicated process. When we speak of proletarian literature not in the sense of particular more or less successful verses or stories, but in the incomparably more weighty sense in which we speak of bourgeois literature, we have no right to forget for one moment the extraordinary cultural backwardness of the overwhelming majority of the proletariat. Art is created on the basis of a continual everyday, cultural, ideological inter-relationship between a class and its artists. Between the aristocracy or the bourgeoisie and their artists there was no split in daily life. The artists lived, and still live, in a bourgeois milieu, breathing the air of bourgeois salons, they received and are receiving hypodermic inspirations from their class. This nourishes the subconscious processes of their creativity. Does the proletariat of today offer such a cultural-ideological milieu, in which the new artist may obtain, without leaving it in his day-to-day existence, all the inspiration he needs while at the same time mastering the procedures of his craft? No, the working masses are culturally extremely backward; the illiteracy or low level of literacy of the majority of the workers presents in itself a very great obstacle to this. And above all, the proletariat, in so far as it remains a proletariat, is compelled to expend its best forces in political struggle, in restoring the economy, and in meeting elementary cultural needs, fighting against illiteracy, lousiness, syphilis, etc.

Of course, the political methods and revolutionary customs of the proletariat can also be called its culture; but this, in any case, is a sort of culture which is destined to die out as a new, real culture develops. And this new culture will be culture all the more to the extent that the proletariat has ceased to be a proletariat, that is, the more successfully and completely socialist society develops.

Mayakovsky wrote a very powerful piece called *The Thirteen Apostles*, the revolutionariness of which was still rather cloudy and formless. And when this same Mayakovsky decided to swing himself round to the proletarian line, and wrote *150 Million*, he suffered a most frightful rationalistic downfall. This means that in his logic he had outrun his real creative condition. With Pilnyak, as we have said already, a similar disparity is to be observed between his conscious striving and the unconscious processes of creation. To this must be added merely this, that arch-proletarian works also do not in themselves provide the writer in present-day conditions with any guarantees that his creativity will prove to be organically linked with the class. Nor do groupings of proletarian writers provide this guarantee, precisely because the writer, by devoting himself to artistic work, is compelled, in existing conditions, to separate himself from the milieu of his own class and breathe an atmosphere which, after all, is the same as that breathed by the "fellow-travellers". This is just one literary circle among other literary circles.

And as regards future prospects, as they are called, I wanted to say something, but my time is long since up. (**Voices:** *"Please go on!"*) "Give us, at least, some view of the way ahead," comrades come back at me. What does this mean? The **Na Postu** comrades and their allied groups are steering towards a proletarian literature created by the circle method, in a laboratory, so to speak. This way forward I reject absolutely. I repeat once more that it is not possible to put in one historical category feudal, bourgeois and proletarian literature. Such a historical classification is radically false. I spoke about this in my book, and all the objections I have heard seem to me unconvincing and

66

frivolous. Those who talk about proletarian literature seriously and over a long period, who make a platform of proletarian culture, are thinking, where this question is concerned, along the line of a formal analogy with bourgeois culture. The bourgeoisie took power and created its own culture; the proletariat, they think having taken power, will create proletarian culture. But the bourgeoisie is a rich and therefore educated class. Bourgeois culture existed already before the bourgeoisie had formally taken power. The bourgeoisie took power in order to perpetuate its rule. The proletariat in bourgeois society is a propertyless and deprived class, and so it cannot create a culture of its own. Only after taking power does it really become aware of its own frightful cultural backwardness. In order to overcome this it needs to abolish those conditions which keep it in the position of a class, the proletariat. The more we can speak of a new culture in being, the less this will possess a class character. This is the fundamental problem – and the principal difference, in so far as we are arguing about the way forward. Some, starting from the principle of proletarian culture, say: we have in mind only the epoch of transition to socialism – those twenty, thirty, fifty years during which the bourgeois world will be transformed. Can the literature, intended and suitable for the proletariat, which will be created in this period, be called proletarian literature? In any case, we are giving this term "proletarian literature" a totally different meaning from the first, broad meaning we spoke of. But this is not the main problem. This basic feature of the transition period, taken on the international scale, is intense class struggle. Those twenty to thirty years of which we speak will be first and foremost a period of open civil war. And civil war, though preparing the way for the great culture of the future, is in itself extremely unfavourable in its effect on contemporary culture. In its immediate effect October more or less killed literature. Poets and artists fell silent. Was this an accident? No. Long ago it was said: when the sound of weapons is heard, the Muses fall silent. A breathing-space was needed if literature was to revive. It began to revive in our country at the same time as NEP began. Reviving, it

67

at once took on the colouring of the fellow-travellers. It is impossible not to reckon with the facts. The tensest moments, that is, those in which our revolutionary epoch finds its highest expression, are unfavourable for literary, and in general for artistic creation. If revolution begins tomorrow in Germany or in all Europe, will this bring an immediate flowering of proletarian literature? Certainly not. It will weaken and destroy, not expand, artistic creation, for we shall again have to mobilize and arm one and all. And amid the clash of arms, the Muses are silent. (**Cries:** *"Demyan wasn't silent."*) Yes, you keep harping on Demyan, but it won't do. You begin by proclaiming a new era of proletarian literature, you create circles, associations, groups for this literature, you again and again refer to Demyan. But Demyan is a product of the old, pre-October literature. He has not founded any school, nor will he found any. He was brought up on Krylov, Gogol and Nekrasov. In this sense he is the revolutionary last-born child of our old literature. The very fact of your referring to him is a refutation of your theory.

What is the way forward? Fundamentally, it is the growth of literacy, education, special courses for workers, the cinema, the gradual reconstruction of everyday life, the further advance in the cultural level. This is the fundamental process, intersecting with new intensifications of civil war, on an all-European and world scale. On this basis, the line of purely literary creation will be an extremely zigzag one. **Kuznitsa**, **Oktyabr** and other such groups are in no sense landmarks along the road of the cultural class creativity of the proletariat, but merely episodes of a superficial nature. If from these groups a few good young poets or writers emerge, this won't give us proletarian literature, but it will be useful. But if you try to transform MAPP and VAPP into factories of proletarian literature, you will certainly fail, just as you have failed up to now. A member of one of these associations regards himself as, in one way, a representative of the proletariat in the world of art, in another way as a representative of art in the world of the proletariat. Membership of VAPP confers a sort of title. It

68

is objected that VAPP is only a Communist circle in which a young poet obtains the necessary inspiration, and so on. Well, and what about the Party? If he is a real poet and a genuine Communist, the Party in all its work will give him incomparably more inspiration than MAPP and VAPP. Of course, the Party must and will pay very great attention to every young artistic talent that is akin or ideologically close to it. But its fundamental task in relation to literature and culture is raising the level of literacy – simple literacy, political literacy, scientific literacy – of the working masses, and thereby laying the foundation for a new art.

I know that this prospect does not satisfy you. It seems insufficiently definite. Why? Because you envisage the further development of culture in too regular, too evolutionary a way: the present shoots of proletarian literature will, you think, grow and develop, becoming continually richer, and so genuine proletarian literature will be created, which later will change into socialist literature. No, things won't develop like that. After the present breathing-space, when a literature strongly coloured by the "fellow-travellers" is being created – not by the Party, not by the state – there will come a period of new, terrible spasms of civil war. We shall inevitably be drawn into it. It is quite possible that revolutionary poets will give us martial verses, but the continuity of literary development will nevertheless be sharply broken. All forces will be concentrated on the direct struggle. Shall we then have a second breathing-space? I do not know. But the result of this new, much mightier period of civil war, if we are victorious, will be the complete securing and consolidation of the socialist basis of our economy. We shall receive fresh technical and organizational help. Our development will go forward at a different rate. And on that basis, after the zigzags and upheavals of civil war, only then will begin a real building of culture, and, consequently, also the creation of a new literature. But this will be socialist culture, built entirely on constant intercourse between the artist and the masses who will have come of age culturally, linked by ties of solidarity. You do not proceed in your thinking from *this* vision of the future: you have your own, the vision of a group. You want our party, in the name of the proletariat, to officially adopt your little artistic factory. You think that, having planted a kidney-bean in a flower pot, you are capable of raising the tree of proletarian literature. That is not the way. No tree can be grown from a kidney-bean.

www.ingramcontent.com/pod-product-compliance
Lightning Source LLC
Chambersburg PA
CBHW060212290526
45789CB00003B/1241